U.N.L.E.A.S.H.E.D.
Destiny

Rochelle D. Jacobs

U.N.L.E.A.S.H.E.D. **Destiny**
© 2024 by Rochelle D. Jacobs All rights reserved.

No part of this publication may be reproduced, distributed, or transmitted in any form or by any means, including photocopying, recording, or other electronic or mechanical methods, without the prior written permission of the publisher, except in the case of brief quotations embodied in critical reviews and certain other noncommercial uses permitted by copyright law.

Dedication

This book is dedicated to the Woman of Faith seeking the freedom to reclaim the power of her voice to speak with power, walk on purpose and live in prosperity and peace.

Beloved, Your Destiny Awaits!

Forward

When Rochelle D. Jacobs extended the invitation for me to write the foreword to her first solo project *"**Unleashed Destiny**"*, I immediately said yes, little knowing the profound impact it would have on me. Reading through the transformative pages of this book, I found myself deeply moved, inspired, and empowered. I have no doubt you will too.

Reflecting on our shared journey, it's clear that the catalyst for our deeper connection was the pandemic—a time that, paradoxically, represented both the worst and the best of times for us all. It was during this period of global uncertainty that I was inspired to create a space aimed at supporting women's overall wellbeing, leading to the inception of **The Reset Challenge**. It was here, during the challenge, that Rochelle D. Jacobs stepped into herself, a woman transformed, driven by a newfound purpose to alter her life and, ultimately, her destiny.

"***Unleashed Destiny,***" is not merely a narrative of Rochelle's life; it is a comprehensive guide designed to empower you to craft the life you truly deserve.

This book is a journey, one that requires your full engagement with pen and highlighter in hand, ready to mark the nuggets and strategies that will serve as your tools for transformation.

Within these pages lies the key to unlocking aspects of your life you may have been unaware needed freeing. You may not have realized it was time to let your hair down, say no to something, shift directions in life, let alone unleash your destiny, until you immerse yourself in this book. Know that you didn't find yourself here by accident. There is divine timing that led you to this moment and this piece of work. Do not take it lightly. Read with curiosity and an open mind to connect to parts of you that are begging for an answer. And if you find yourself asking the question—When does your destiny need an intervention? I'd say the answer is Right Now!

Your Destiny Awaits You!

XOXO,

Dr. Shana

U.N.L.E.A.S.H.E.D. **Destiny**

Rochelle D. Jacobs

Table of Contents

1 | *Introduction*

3 | *Un·leash·ed*

7 | *Un·con·scious*

17 | *Ne·glect*

27 | *Li·es*

37 | *(ε)*

49 | *Ad·dic·tion*

61 | *Strong·hold*

71 | *Heal·ing*

75 | *Ex·traor·di·nar·y*

83 | *Des·tin·y*

90 | *Important Help lines and Websites*

Introduction
U.N.L.E.A.S.H.E.D.

Beloved, thank you for investing in Your Destiny! I will share insights and strategies that will help you identify and overcome fears, so that you will step out of your comfort zone and embrace new opportunities. While you read this book, you must be comfortable with being uncomfortable while you honestly and bravely confront and heal from feelings of shame. You will learn to identify and transform your limiting beliefs to pursue your dreams with renewed vigor and determination. *"Unleashed Destiny"* is a transformative guide for the woman of faith seeking to unleash her true potential and live a more empowered and fulfilling life.

- Are you living in the shackles of your fears?
- Do you have the confidence and clarity you need to create the results you desire NOW?
- Are you ready to dismantle and replace your dysfunctional patterns?
- It's time to unleash your power to create the extraordinary life YOU desire.

Becoming unleashed is about the energy you hold. Everything carries energy, which is why you must manifest what you're committed to! When you become unleashed, you have a magnetic energy that consumes you, to not only attract what you want in life, but also keep it! Becoming unleashed means being ready for what you want, and then being able to actually receive it. Imagine what could be possible if you had the freedom to really be yourself?

Imagine what could be manifested for you if you stopped allowing your fears and doubts to win the game? Once you become unleashed, you'll stop experiencing the frustration that dysfunctional experiences create. Once and for all you'll begin to experience the JOY that comes from creating and having everything you want and deserve.

Imagine how amazing THAT will be! If you are 100% ready and committed to breaking free from your past, ready to release your magnetic essence, and claim the life you want – LET'S BECOME UNLEASHED!

Un·leash·ed

Un·leash
- to release from a leash or restraint, to loose
- to set free from restraints
- to throw, shoot, or set in motion forcefully
- to suddenly release a violent force that cannot be controlled

January 1, 2017 *"unleashed"* was my focus word. My Destiny needed an Intervention so that I can get clear of my personal, professional and power goals. Because I was drifting through life unconscious, I could not identify obstacles that restrained me from attaining those goals as well as seeking strategies for overcoming those obstacles.

Have you ever wanted more out of your life, but you didn't know where to start?

Through constant learning and self-evaluation, I invite you as you read this book to seek and crave these simple steps that I took to start to unleash my own potential.

Beloved, inside this book, you will discover powerful, yet simple steps to becoming the best version of **You**!

- Understand Yourself - identifying strengths and weaknesses (**Superpowers**)
- Importance of Communication - internal and external communication
- 12 Dimensions of becoming Wholly Well
- Developing Yourself - importance of coaches, mentors, and accountability partners
- Investing in Yourself - setting BIG life goals, strategies, and reaping big dividends of ROI's (return of investments)

My real-life stories will assist you in making a connection with **You** and how **You** can find your way to **unleash** your potential. The first step begins with self-awareness, being vulnerable, and being confident in who you are. It is scary but incredibly powerful.

The next step to **unleashing** your potential revolves around how you speak to yourself and others. How you communicate with yourself is often overlooked and changing how you speak to yourself internally and externally will impact your life. The third step is the importance of not delegating your professional and per-

-sonal development to other people but being the driving force behind it. As my beloved wellness coach, **Dr. Shana teaches; "Sis, ain't n-o-b-o-d-y coming to save you!"** Self-learning is not the only critical aspect in development but also taking advantage of coaches, mentors, tribes, and a confidante. The fourth and final step is setting the proper course. You will read specifics on setting BIG goals and the importance of setting proper strategies, and tactics to accomplish more than you have in the past. There is never a finish line to unleashing your potential because every day we should be striving to learn and grow, and these four areas can become a way of life for you just like they have for me.

Did you know you have a superpower, but you haven't tapped into it yet? Maybe you're scared to use it or maybe you don't even know what your superpower is. What if I told you that you could tap into your superpower and start achieving the success you've always wanted? With a little help, you can finally unleash your inner power and start living the life of your dreams and start using your power to make a difference in the world.

If you are a CEO, solo-preneur, aspiring entrepreneur or a soccer mom wanting to live life to the fullest...I'm going to cut right to the chase.

There's a massive opportunity in the marketplace right now for great women coaches, in all areas and niches... leadership, speaking, personal development, executive coaching, organization, productivity, unleashing your passion, specialized skill sets...you name it. The demand right now is extremely high, especially post-pandemic, where women of faith now recognize they can do more with their lives and their innate gifts than making their bosses rich.

The truth of the matter is I have been walking around for the last 20 years unconscious, hiding from who I could become. During the pandemic, the time came to *unleash* my creative energy to propel me into a new era. My **destiny** has been *unleashed* as I continue to invest in my own personal wellness through transformation in mind, body, and spirit.

Un·con·scious

not conscious; done or existing without one realizing; unaware of...

"The conscious mind determines the actions; the unconscious mind determines the reactions; and the reactions are just as important as the actions."
—E. Stanley Jones

"A life lived of choice is a life of conscious action. A life lived of chance is a life of unconscious creation.
—Neale Donald Walsch

Unconsciousness is a state in which a living individual exhibits a complete, or near-complete inability to maintain an awareness of self and environment or to respond to any human or environmental stimulus; a state without control of one's own actions.

The unconscious mind has been viewed as an enemy, a murky power that swooped in to sabotage our conscious desires. It has become the scapegoat for every failure, mistake, or unwanted reaction.

When I reflect on the unconscious mind, I see that it preserves the body.

One of its main objectives is the survival of your physical body. The unconscious mind will fight anything that appears to be a threat to that survival. So, if you want to change a behavior more easily, show your unconscious how that behavior is hurting your body.

The unconscious mind also communicates through emotion and symbols. To get your attention, the unconscious uses emotions. For example, if you suddenly feel afraid, your unconscious has detected (right or wrong) that your survival is at risk.

I grew up in the 3rd Ward area (the Cuney Homes), amidst the ebb and flow of life in Houston, Texas. I lived with my grandmother. I soon discovered I was not like other girls who appeared to have it all together with confidence and clarity. Instead, I glided through my paltry life in a state of perpetual unconsciousness, drifting through many days with a vacant stare and a faint smile that never quite reached my eyes.

I was a mystery to those around me. I spent countless days at the local library, where I would spend days lost in the pages of novels, my mind wandering through the words, but never truly grasping their meaning. Girls would often whisper about my strange demeanor, speculating about what might be going on inside my head. I was unaware of their curiosity. I existed in a world of my own making, where reality and dreams intertwined seamlessly. Yet, there were moments when reality would intrude upon my reverie, like cracks in a fragile facade. I would catch glimpses of my reflection in the window of the library to the outside world, feeling empty and distant, and for a fleeting instant, I would feel a pang of something akin to sadness, though I couldn't quite name it.

One day, lost in a daydream, the librarian stopped by my table. She smiled and looked at me, with eyes that seemed to see straight through my facade. "Excuse me," she said softly, "But I couldn't help but notice you sitting here. You seem lost in thought." I blinked, slowly returning to the present moment. I gazed at her with a mixture of curiosity and wariness. "I suppose I am," I replied, my voice barely more than a whisper. She smiled gently. "I know what it's like to feel lost," she said. But sometimes, all it takes is a gentle nudge to find your way back." And with that, she handed me a book by Judy Blume, <u>Are You There God? It's Me, Margaret</u>, its pages filled with words that seemed to dance across the page. I accepted the book with trembling hands, my heart fluttering in my chest. As I went to check out I asked the librarian, "How many books am I allowed to check out?" When she replied as many as I liked, my love for reading took on new heights!!! For the first time in what felt like an eternity, I found myself truly awake. As I began reading books like *Nancy Drew & the Hardy Boys*, *Little House on the Prairie* and *Dr. Seuss*, I felt a spark ignite within me—a flicker of recognition, of understanding, of something resembling life. From that day forward, I began to awaken from my unconscious state. With each turn of the pages of my cache of books, I discovered new depths within myself, new dreams to chase and new realities to explore. And though the journey was not always easy, I knew that I was no longer alone—that as long as there were words to guide me, I would never truly be lost again.

To the outside world, I appeared to be a picture of having not a care in the world, but beneath the surface, I carried a burden that weighed heavy on my soul—a trauma so deep-rooted— that left me trapped in a state of unconsciousness, unable to fully face the pain that lingered within. At night, when the world grew quiet and still, I would lie awake in bed, haunted by fragments of memories that flickered at the edge of consciousness. I would toss and turn, trying in vain to escape the ghosts that lurked in the shadows of my, but try as I might, I could not outrun the echoes of my past forever. They followed me like a shadow, a constant reminder of the pain I had buried deep within my heart. I share this trauma that was stemmed from a dark chapter in my past—a chapter I had long tried to bury beneath layers of denial and avoidance in my anthology book, <u>"When **Destiny Needs An Intervention**", Volume 3"</u>; *"For the Love of Brokenness"*. It was a memory I dared not confront, for fear of the raw emotions. It would stir within me—the guilt, the shame, the pain of being sexually molested. I went days and years in a haze, going through the motions of life without truly living. I would smile when appropriate and nod when spoken to, but my mind was always elsewhere, lost in a fog of numbness and detachment. It was the call for authors by my beloved Visionary and Executive Wellness coach, Dr. Shana D. Lewis that I began seeking solace and healing from my state of unconsciousness.

As I began investing in myself through Dr. Shana's YXL (Your Extraordinary Life) Academy, I found myself putting in the work to transform my story of courage, of resilience, of healing. Inspired by the prompting of my midwife, my beloved writing coach, Crystal Cunningham, I began to confront and own my demons, one painful memory at a time.

I sought out therapy, opening up to a compassionate therapist who helped me to navigate the labyrinth of my overwhelming emotions. I reached out to loved ones and my sisterhood of Destiny Diamonds, finding comfort and support in their unwavering presence. And most importantly, I learned to forgive myself—to acknowledge that I was not defined by my past, but rather by the strength and courage it took to overcome it.

For the first time, I began to see glimpses of my own reflection in the words I wrote by sharing my story, as if a light had been cast upon the darkest corners of my soul. *"For the Love of Brokenness"* is a story of fear, pain, and shame. There is a powerful transformation that will create a stirring within, a flicker of hope, of possibility, and the promise of a brighter tomorrow. After writing my chapter, I realized that I was not alone in my brokenness—that there are women- wives, mothers, daughters, and sisters, who are walking on a similar path and will emerge on the other side, stronger and more resilient than before. As the days turned into weeks and the weeks into months, my unconscious state began to lift, like a veil being lifted from my eyes.

My destiny and way of thinking became crystal clear! I no longer felt imprisoned by my trauma, but rather liberated by the knowledge that I was the authority of sharing and telling my own signature story—a story of survival, of resilience, of triumph over adversity, and though the scars of my past would always remain, I knew that my hardships and challenges were a testament to the battles I had fought and the victories I had won. In facing my demons head-on, I discovered the most powerful truth of all—that even in the darkest of nights, there is always a glimmer of light, waiting to guide me to my **Destiny**.

It's time to arise beloved Queen! Unconsciousness stores and organizes memories. The unconscious decides where and how your memories are stored. It may hide certain memories (such as traumas) that have strong negative emotions until you are mature enough to process them consciously. When it senses that you are ready (whether you consciously think you are or not), it will bring them up so you can deal with them. The unconscious absorbs pictures rather than words. It does not process negatives, so if you say; "I don't want to procrastinate," the unconscious generates a picture of you procrastinating.

Switching that picture from the negative to the positive takes an extra step. It is better to tell your unconscious, **"Let's get to work!"**

The unconscious makes associations and learns quickly. To protect you, the unconscious stays alert and tries to glean the lessons from each experience. For example, if you had a bad experience in school, your unconscious may choose to lump all your learning experiences into the **"this is not going to be fun"** category. It will signal you with sweaty palms and anxiety whenever you attempt something new, but if you do well in sports, your unconscious will remember that *"sports equals success"* and you'll feel positive and energized whenever physical activity comes up.

There's much more to the unconscious mind. In fact, my stories in this book will focus on the unconscious, how it works, and how to deal with it. Even just understanding the basics above, will help you harness its power. If you're feeling stuck, it can help to first identify your reasons, and then figure out what works to help you remove your roadblocks.

10 Techniques
to free yourself from a state of unconsciousness

1. Mindfulness Meditation:
Practice mindfulness by focusing on your breath, sensations, and thoughts

2. Journaling:
Write down your thoughts, feelings, and experiences regularly

3. Gratitude Practice:
Daily gratitude exercises can shift your focus to positive aspects of your life, fostering a greater sense of awareness and appreciation

4. Breath work:
Engaging in deep, conscious breathing exercises can help you reconnect with your body and the
present moment, reducing stress and increasing awareness

5. Body Scan:
Perform a body scan meditation, where you systematically focus on and relax each part of your body

6. Mindful Movement:
Engage in activities like yoga, tai chi, or walking meditation

7. Observation:
Spend time observing your surroundings and the people around you without judgment

8. Self-Inquiry:
Ask yourself probing questions about your beliefs, emotions, and actions

9. Digital Detox:
Limit your use of digital devices and social media to reduce distractions and increase your ability to be present in the moment

10. Mindful Listening:
Practice active listening in your conversations, fully focusing on the speaker without planning your response

Conclusion

By implementing these techniques consistently you become empowered to break free from unconscious patterns and live a more conscious, present, and fulfilling life.

Ne·glect

"I have no sound, just silence. No cause for being myself. I have no offering to make except grief and sorrow. You may not in an instant call me by name, but surely you are personally acquainted with me." My name is **Neglect!!!!**

It has been said that "he who neglects the present moment throws away all he has." How tragic it is to find that an entire lifetime is wasted in pursuit of distractions while your purpose is being neglected! The definition of neglect is simply to fail to care for someone or something properly. It leads to mistreatment due to a lack of attention. It can also be active neglect, which is intentional, or passive neglect, which is from a lack of experience, information, or ability.

I have intended no evil, but because my talents have come to nothingness, courtesy and kindness have failed, and the promise of success and happiness has yielded sorrow and disaster."

—Author Unknown

Beloved, do you find yourself in a state of neglect because you were never told your value? What are you neglecting? Health? Family? Self-care? Finances?

Neglect was a major reason for some of the most painful experiences I suffered in life. As I look back over my life as the 2nd oldest daughter, I often felt a deep sense of loneliness and sadness. My mom and stepfather were both constantly caught up in the whirlwind of their dysfunctional lives. They loved me and my sisters but were perpetually busy, arguing and fighting, leaving little time for me and my sisters. I am thankful for the lessons learned from them like, don't get pregnant, and the importance of getting a good education. So from a young age, I learned to fend for myself. The neglect of love by my mom and stepdad left me emotionally distant and absorbed in my own world. I spent most of my time engrossed in television shows or reading books, using these activities to escape feelings of neglect, inadequacy and depression. I often felt like I was walking on eggshells. Fridays were my favorite day of the week because I got an allowance to spend on sugary sweets.

School was my refuge. I loved being in the student council and found solace in the structured classroom environment. My teachers always noticed my diligence and intelligence, often praising my hard work.

I kept my home life a secret, too ashamed to let anyone know about the chaos there. My friendships with girls were very superficial. I preferred hanging out with the boys instead. I feared letting anyone get too close and discovering the truth about my family.

Before my 5th grade graduation, my stepfather died, so we had to move from our home. I remember our next-door neighbor came over to meet us and invited us to go to church with her and her family. She made me feel valued and loved. Soon I began to open up about my neglect and the dysfunction at home, never having enough food to eat, or our electricity often being cut off. My sisters and I would cower and hide while hearing our mom being abused by her new boyfriend. My church family became a pivotal influence in my life. Through the nurtured bible classes, youth conferences and rap sessions, I learned how to express healthy emotions and develop friendships. I also started to understand that my mom's behavior was a reflection of her unresolved issues, not a measure of my self-worth, and so, my story is a testament to the power of care and attention, showing that even the smallest acts of kindness shown by my neighbor and church family can make a profound difference!

As an adult, I began neglecting my health, family, self-care, and finances with emotional stress eating.

I felt like the Tasmanian devil, seeking sugary sweets to self-soothe the hurt, shame, and fear within me. I would often find myself in my garage standing in my robe eating a dozen, yes you read that right (12) cookies and cream ice cream sandwiches. I became a pathological sweet demon, secretly hiding and eating sugary sweets to fill the deep void created by the emotional trauma of neglect I had endured in my life.

The sugar struggle was real, and I needed that surge of dopamine to feel better, to cope with those feelings of pain, worry, depression, heavy heartedness, and discouragement. After waking from my state of unconsciousness, I saw myself walking on a road headed on a journey to nowhere. I needed an intervention – and it was fast approaching. In each direction I would go, I encountered unexpected obstacles and challenges. I tried on my own to adapt to new circumstances and the choices I had to make along the way. At the end of this barren road, I began to embrace the power of resilience, resourcefulness, and the courage required to forge ahead when the path is unclear. I learned valuable lessons about perseverance and the importance of seeking guidance and support from unexpected sources.

I discovered a passion for writing, using my journal as a safe space to pour out my thoughts and feelings. The best investment I have ever made has been in myself, by becoming a member of the YXL (Your Extraordinary Life) Academy, where I found a supportive community and sisterhood of **Destiny** Diamonds.

Over time my life has been transformed, the neglect I once felt was replaced with love and attention. I stand today in a place of being not only a survivor but thriving personally, professionally, spiritually, and emotionally, knowing that I am cherished and valued.

Today, I decide to free myself from this place of neglect surrounded by unfamiliar faces and places. Looking at myself in the mirror, I did not recognize the woman I had become. Navigating my new path from neglect to nurture is pivotal in my journey. I began giving attention, care, and consideration to my mind, body, and spirit, therefore illustrating the transformative power of stepping out of my comfort zone and embracing the adventure of my *Unleashed* **Destiny.** The moment I was unleashed, a surge of liberation coursed through me, shattering the chains that had bound my creativity. Like a wild stallion set free, I galloped across the open fields of my creative imagination, my thoughts racing with a newfound kinetic energy. The weight of restraint lifted, allowing my words to flow like a torrential river, carving intricate paths through the untouched landscapes of possibility.

Every sentence in this book became a brushstroke on the canvas of existence, and with each stroke, I painted a masterpiece of unrestrained expression. As a member of Karla Aghedo's H3W (Houston Wellness Workshops for Women), participating in her Boss Ladies Mastermind Group has been a game-changer for me. The insight and breakthrough I experienced during the sessions are profound. So often I feel the chains of fear, neglect, and self-doubt start to loosen their grip on my spirit. The support and wisdom shared by the group and our facilitator provided me with new tools and perspectives to overcome my challenges. I am now more empowered and confident, ready to walk in my true power. These master classes have truly been a pivotal investment in my transformational journey. Freeing yourself from the grip of neglect, especially if it has been a part of your life for a long time, is a challenging but achievable journey.

12 Steps
to heal and move forward

1. Acknowledge and Validate Your Feelings
Recognize that neglect is a form of abuse and that your feelings of pain and worthlessness are valid. Understand that the neglect you experienced is not your fault and does not define your worth.

2. Seek Professional Help
Consider therapy or counseling to work through the emotional scars of neglect. A professional can help you understand your experiences and develop healthy coping mechanisms. Look for therapists who specialize in trauma and neglect to get the most appropriate support.

3. Build a Support Network
Surround yourself with supportive and understanding people who can offer emotional support and encouragement. Join support groups where you can share your experiences and hear from others who have faced similar challenges.

4. Practice Self-Care
Engage in activities that promote your well-being, such as exercise, healthy eating, and sufficient sleep. Take time for hobbies and interests that bring you joy and help you relax.

5. Develop Self-Compassion
Be kind to yourself and practice self-compassion. Recognize that healing is a process and allow yourself to feel and process your emotions without judgment. Challenge negative self-talk and replace it with affirmations and positive self-talk.

6. Set Boundaries
Learn to set healthy boundaries with people who may still be neglectful or toxic. This includes limiting contact or completely distancing yourself from those who continue to cause harm. Assert your needs and make it clear what behavior is acceptable and what is not.

7. Educate Yourself
Read books and articles about neglect and its effects to better understand what you've been through and how to heal. Knowledge can empower you to make informed decisions about your healing process.

8. Cultivate New Relationships
Build new, healthy relationships that are based on mutual respect and care. Seek out friends and partners who are supportive, attentive, and nurturing.

9. Focus on Personal Growth
Set personal goals and work towards achieving them. This can help you build a sense of accomplishment and self-worth. Engage in activities that help you grow, such as education, volunteering, or pursuing new skills.

10. Practice Mindfulness and Meditation
Engage in mindfulness and meditation practices to help you stay grounded in the present moment and manage anxiety and stress. These practices can help you develop greater self-awareness and emotional regulation.

11. Explore Creative Outlets
Use creative outlets like writing, art, or music to express your emotions and experiences. Creativity can be a powerful tool for processing and healing from past neglect.

12. Reclaim Your Narrative
Recognize that you have the power to rewrite your story. Focus on your strengths and achievements rather than your past neglect. Embrace the idea that you can create a fulfilling and happy life despite the challenges you've faced.

Conclusion

Healing from neglect is a journey that requires patience, support, and self-compassion. By taking these steps, you can begin to free yourself from the grip of neglect and build a life filled with love, respect, and fulfillment. Remember, beloved, it's okay to seek help and take the time you need to heal.

Li·es

Lies are intentional false statements known to be untrue.

"Lies are like scars on your soul. They destroy you."
— Lana Winters

"A single lie discovered is enough to create doubt in every truth expressed."
— Unknown

"Every lie is two lies—the lie we tell others and the lie we tell ourselves to justify it."
— Robert Brault

From a very young age, my story about destiny was a story filled with lies. I believed that my life was destined for scarcity and lack, and that I would always endure hardship, never to rise above my circumstances. I would often question why God put me here on earth when eventually I would die. So what was the point of dreaming and imagining? I should just live life barely without any goals or vision. But God reminds me in Proverbs 29:18 "Where there is no vision, the people perish." So, after being baptized into Christ at the age of

12, I now stand on His promise in Jeremiah 29:11 "For I know the plans I have for you," declares the Lord, "plans to prosper you and not to harm you, plans to give you hope and a future."

I felt a spark of something greater within me as I read countless books at my local library, about tales of adventure, magic, and far-off places. Each story ignited my imagination and filled me with a sense of longing and possibility. Everywhere I went - church, work, school, my friends' houses I would dream and imagine a life beyond the horizon.

As I grew older, after the death of my stepfather and later my mother, and after I graduated from High School in 1990, the lies about my **destiny** began to weigh heavily on me. Lies like, **"You will be like your mother and have babies out of wedlock. No man will want to marry a skinny, molested, pathetic girl like you."** No money, no home, no savings, no good credit, no career - all these lies echoed in my mind, creating a tug-of-war between my dreams and the belief that I was destined for a paltry life. Oh wretched girl, who do you think you are that you deserve an Extraordinary Life?

As life continued to give me lemons, I realized that I have the power to create my own path, and I give myself the authority to write my own signature story.

My **Destiny** is shaped by my choices, my beliefs, and my actions. If I continue to believe in the lies of Satan: (the Father of Lies) who only wants to kill, steal, and destroy, they will become a stronghold.

Beloved reader, **"Today you get to decide to believe in your dreams and that you possess the power to transform your life."**

How did I begin my own transformation? I started by owning my mistakes and started holding myself accountable. I realized that no one was coming to save me or just hand me my destiny. I would guard time each day to pursue my passions—journaling and writing stories, learning new skills, and even going back to school to earn my undergraduate degree at Texas Southern University in Houston, Texas, Go Tigers!

I started saving and investing in ME. As I sit here writing this story, I am overcome with such grace, mercy, and thankfulness for the God that I serve. My small investments have reaped BIG rewards. The truth about lies encompasses their nature, impact, and the reasons behind them. Lies can take many forms, from minor falsehoods to significant deceptions, and they can have far-reaching consequences for individuals and society.

Here are my key insights into the truth about lies:

Lie # 1: Separation from God

I remember, in 2018, I was asked to co-teach a women's bible study by Beth Moore: *A Woman's Heart*. Satan's lies created a barrier between my faith in God, leading me on a barren, wilderness road of spiritual alienation. The question that God asked Adam in Genesis 3: 9, "Where are you?" really spoke to my heart. I felt so distant from God's presence and struggled with feelings of guilt, shame, and unworthiness. I believed the lies about my identity and worth of living in poverty and lack and it led to my distorted self-image. How did I end up here? I suffered from low self-esteem, self-hatred, and a lack of confidence that was preventing me from living up to my full potential. Who am I to teach other women, and I needed a heart check? Satan's lies began to blur the lines between right and wrong, leading to the moral confusion of making hurtful and harmful decisions.

Lie # 2: Fear and Anxiety

Lies that instill fear and anxiety began to paralyze me and prevented me from taking positive actions. I found myself parked at a place called **"Chronic Stress and Worry"** which soon lead to my mental health issue of being **"Depressed."** I became a best performing actress at the **"Life of Hypocrisy!"**

Pretending that I was ok, when deep down I was a hot mess. I would smile in public but behind closed doors I cried myself to sleep daily! I would binge on sugary sweets to numb the fear and anxiety.

This stress soon manifested, and I developed a pain in my side that wouldn't go away. My marital relationship was filled with deceptive lies that created mistrust and conflict with my husband. In 2010, I found out that my husband lied to me about a family member of his. That lie was very damaging and destroyed our relationship with its deceit and betrayal. You've heard the expression, "hurt people, hurt people." Well, I took it to another level with my sugar addiction and destructive behaviors, desperately seeking happiness or relief to fill the void of my brokenness that only led to further misery and bondage.

I soon became a deceitful liar! I was living in a place of scarcity. Working and living paycheck to paycheck! I would spend money on sugary sweets instead of paying my bills. Then hid pink slips and cancellation notices hoping my husband wouldn't find out how bad I was at being a poor steward of our finances. As I sit here in my uncomfortable shame, low self-esteem, vulnerability, insecurity, and loss of independence, my stinking thinking was to hurt him with his credit to get him back for lying to me!

I soon found out that I was only hurting myself. As I reflected on my choices, I realized that my lies may comfort me for a little while, but the truth always empowers me. God has delivered me from this fear not to forget everything and run, but to face everything and rise!

Lie #3: Hindered Spiritual Growth

The Lies of Satan stunted my spiritual growth and kept me focused on falsehoods rather than truth. From 2010 until 2017, I struggled to grow in my faith, lacking the guidance and peace that comes from a close relationship with God. Satan's lies promoted despair and hopelessness that robbed me of hope and motivation. I forgot about my dreams and aspirations along the way. I felt that positive change was impossible. So, I isolated myself from my family and friends. I didn't feel worthy of love or anyone's trust. I was running on a hamster wheel, going nowhere fast. My season of isolation exacerbated feelings of loneliness, depression, and hopelessness, creating a vicious cycle of disconnection. The lies of Satan, distorted my truth, created chaos, and lead me away from God's love and purpose for my life, but I soon came to myself having a prodigal daughter moment of clarity.

Satan's lies:

Deceit	Hypocrisy	Unworthiness
Secrets	Dishonesty	Distrust
Deception	Hurt	Selfishness
Betrayal	Disrespect	Negativity

I recognized and rejected the lies through building my faith, fasting, praying, and studying scripture because it became crucial to maintaining my spiritual health and well-being. By seeking truth and fostering a relationship with God, I am a "Comeback Champion" of the destructive effects of these lies and I am living a more fulfilled, fruitful, and faithful life.

10 Steps
to help you break free from Satan's Lies

1. **Know the Truth**
   - **Study the Bible:** Regularly read and study the Bible to understand God's truth and promises. Scriptures like John 8:32 ("Then you will know the truth, and the truth will set you free") emphasize the power of truth.
   - **Meditate on God's Word:** Reflect on key Bible verses that affirm your identity in Christ, God's love, and His plans for you.

2. **Strengthen Your Faith**
   - **Pray Regularly:** Communicate with God through prayer, seeking His guidance, strength, and protection against lies.
   - **Join a Faith Community:** Engage with a church or small group where you can receive support, accountability, and encouragement.

3. **Renew Your Mind**
   - **Challenge Negative Thoughts:** Identify and challenge negative thoughts and lies with biblical truth. Replace lies with affirmations based on scripture.
   - **Practice Gratitude:** Focus on gratitude to shift your mindset from negativity to positivity, recognizing God's blessings in your life.

4. **Seek Accountability and Support**
   - **Confide in Trusted Believers:** Share your struggles with trusted friends, mentors, or spiritual leaders who can pray for you and offer wise counsel.
   - **Attend Counseling:** Consider Christian counseling to address deep-rooted issues and receive professional support.

5. **Armor Yourself Spiritually**
   - **Put on the Full Armor of God:** Ephesians 6:10-18 describes the armor of God (truth, righteousness, peace, faith, salvation, and the Word of God) that protects you against spiritual attacks.
   - **Stay Vigilant:** Be aware of the enemy's tactics and remain alert to spiritual warfare.

6. **Cultivate a Life of Worship**
   - **Worship God Regularly**: Engage in worship through singing, praise, and thanksgiving, which helps to refocus your heart and mind on God.
   - **Live a Godly Life**: Strive to live according to biblical principles, demonstrating integrity, love, and humility.

7. **Serve Others**
   - **Practice Compassion:** Serve others in your community and church, reflecting Christ's love and breaking the focus on yourself.
   - **Use Your Gifts:** Identify and use your spiritual gifts to glorify God and help others find purpose and fulfillment.

8. **Forgive and Let Go**
   - **Forgive Others:** Release any bitterness or unforgiveness, which can be used by the enemy to keep you in bondage.
   - **Forgive Yourself:** Accept God's forgiveness and forgive yourself for past mistakes, embracing a new beginning in Christ.

9. **Stay Connected to the Holy Spirit**
   - **Be Led by the Spirit:** Seek the guidance of the Holy Spirit in your daily life, allowing Him to direct your steps and reveal truth to you.
   - **Cultivate Spiritual Disciplines:** Practice spiritual disciplines such as fasting, solitude, and silence to deepen your relationship with God.

10. **Declare Your Freedom**
    - **Speak Life:** Verbally declare your freedom from the lies of Satan, using scriptures that affirm your identity and victory in Christ.
    - **Stand Firm**: Stand firm in your faith, knowing that Christ has already won the victory over sin and deception (1 Corinthians 15:57).

Conclusion

Freeing yourself from the "**Lies of Satan**" requires a combination of spiritual growth, mental renewal, and practical actions rooted in faith and God's Word. By knowing the truth, strengthening your faith, renewing your mind, and living a life dedicated to God, you can overcome these lies and walk in the freedom and purpose that God has for you.

(ε)

Ep·si·lon
The epsilon symbol is versatile and its meaning varies significantly across different scientific, mathematical, and technical fields. Its general theme tends to revolve around small quantities, precision, and tolerance.

Ex·pen·sive
Something is high priced or costs a lot of money, time, effort or sacrifice....

"**M**y expensive lifestyle led to unwanted consequences like overspending, having no savings, being unprepared for emergencies, falling into debt, and being unable to retire. When you're out of alignment with God's will, expenses open you up to stress and other related health problems. So, I had to answer a tough question, of whether or not I have expensive habits. My greed for sugary sweets became more expensive than eating healthy. All the lies I told and the cost of my integrity was way too expensive. I realized that the cheapest thing in life was money; the most expensive thing was my self-love and self-responsibility. My expensive pleasures caused me to crash and burn. It's a sneaky situation, how did I end up here with this STD? (Sugary Transmitted Disease) Help! I need a doctor, please! My obsession with scarcity had me taking for granted the very things that my survival depended on—air, water, climate, food, safety, even my relationships. My destiny needed an intervention when I realized that something as critically important as my wellness became scarce and hence expensive. I had to change my mind-set and begin to acknowledge my value. Today, I embrace **Freedom,** which to me, is an expensive gift always worth fighting for. *"I never knew the weight until I felt the freedom."*

"In mathematics, epsilon represents a small, seemingly insignificant quantity. It's used to describe limits and define continuity. Though it appears minor, epsilon is crucial for ensuring precision and understanding the true nature of functions."

Similarly, in life, the small, often overlooked moments and actions hold immense significance. They are the building blocks of our destiny." I realized that MY life, filled with material excess, was devoid of these meaningful moments. My pursuit of luxury had overshadowed the smaller, yet more significant aspects of life that truly contribute to a sense of purpose and fulfillment.

I decided to make a change. I accepted a Reset Challenge that was a game changer. Instead of spending money on sugary sweets, I invested in walking, eating healthy fruits and vegetables, and drinking water. I began to simplify my life, by decluttering my closet and other possessions and focused on experiences that brought genuine joy and meaning. Instead of spending money on expensive things I began investing in my mind, body, and spiritual transformation that included:

- Mastermind/Mastermind Groups
- Book Clubs/Ladies Bible Classes
- Strength Gallup Assessment
- ME 2.0 (12 dimensions of wellness)
- Retreats
- Networking Groups

These small, meaningful activities brought a sense of satisfaction and purpose that my formerly expensive lifestyle never could. Each act of kindness, each moment of genuine connection, was like an epsilon in my life—seemingly minor, yet profoundly important in shaping my destiny. As I continue on this journey, I see and feel the transformation within.

I am filled with a deep sense of fulfillment and direction. My relationships have improved, and I have discovered a newfound passion for helping others find their purpose as well.

Beloved, true fulfillment comes not from the grandiose, but from the small, significant actions that define our destiny. Just as epsilon ensures precision and truth in mathematics, these moments ensure a life of purpose and meaning. I pray as you read about my journey illustrated by my past, that you will gain wisdom to understand that an expensive lifestyle, while dazzling on the surface, could never substitute for the deeper satisfaction that comes from living a life of purpose. The epsilon moments seem small yet are very significant, and they are what truly shape our destinies and bring lasting fulfillment."

Emp·ty
the absence of...

Do you ever feel empty because you have not yet encountered your real or authentic self? I have discovered that sometimes we must be empty in order to be vessels for better things. We must become aware of the empty void in order to fill it. The truth of the matter is for a very long time I was not okay at all, but horribly empty. As I continue to fill my cup I now know what it is like to be filled. I have to admit the hard truth-

"I must know nothing before I can learn something and be empty before I can be filled."
– Author Unknown

The profound emptiness that lurked deep within me, that sense of living an empty life without a clear destiny, is no longer a path I am willing to continue upon. Pre-pandemic, my life revolved around taking care of my family, working just to make ends meet and achieving the bare minimum, but I couldn't shake the feeling that something crucial was missing. My existence seemed like an endless sequence of tasks with no deeper meaning, much like an epsilon in a mathematical equation—tiny, almost negligible, and seemingly insignificant. It was a stark contrast to the constant noise and haste of my life.

One evening, in December of 2016, drawn by a sudden impulse and looking forward to walking into the new year a brand new me, I decided to attend a vision board party. I was excited to just go and support my friend in the launch of her new book *"Get Your Life: The 90 Day Journal"*, but as I reflect back on that day I realize it catapulted me towards having a profound journey of an unleashed destiny starting in 2017 until now. This journey was filled with challenges and discoveries. I realized that just as epsilon was crucial in the precise definition of limits and continuity in calcu-

-lus, every small action and decision in my life contributed to my overall *destiny*. Epsilon was not insignificant; it was a vital component that ensured the accuracy and integrity of mathematical truths. These moments were not meaningless—they were the building blocks of towards my *destiny*. Similarly, I discovered that every moment, no matter how trivial it seemed, was essential in shaping MY OWN *destiny*. In my state of emptiness I needed to find my true purpose in these moments and recognize their significance.

Starting in August of 2008, October of 2013 & 2015, then March of 2016, my family and I experienced several deaths of our family members which left a profound sense of emptiness and grief within me. The end of those relationships and the absence of our in-laws and loved ones whom I was very close to, led to feelings of emptiness that I tried to fill with sugary sweets to numb the pain and grief. Self-soothing became an important skill I used for managing my feelings of emptiness, stress, and emotional distress.

Beginning in 2008 until 2010 there was a major life change, an uncomfortable transition with finishing my associates degree from ITT Tech Institute, not working in my field of study (Computer Networking), being unemployed and then dealing with my son having unexplained seizures created a sense of loss and disorientation for me. My unfulfilled dreams and goals of not achieving my personal or professional aspirations that I set for myself after attending the vision board party in 2016, so that I could get my life back on track to walk in my destiny resulted in my feelings of emptiness and disappointment. Then, there was the season of loneliness- those prolonged periods of isolation or lack of meaningful connections with my family and friends that also led to my deep sense of emptiness.

Post-pandemic, we have heard that Mental Health Struggles are a real condition, and I have suffered from depression, anxiety, and complete burnout due to my feelings of emptiness and lack of purpose. My life seemed routine, monotonous, lacked excitement and variety and a sense of emptiness. All of these moments played a part my life experience, and while they were challenging, they *unleashed* my **destiny** of personal growth and transformation in mind, body and spirit. Inspired by this revelation, I viewed my life through a new lens.

I am now actively hosting an accountability group helping women of faith with unleashing their own destinies. I am a collective member of the SisStore Joy bookstore and have cultivated a circle of sisters who share my love for living, learning and leading.

I have discovered a passion for writing books and hosting podcasts, something I did envision for my life.

As I embrace these small moments and activities, I feel a wholly burst of fulfillment and purpose. My life, which felt empty, is now filled with meaning. I no longer see myself as a tiny, insignificant epsilon, but as a vital part of the larger equation of life. Every interaction, every act of kindness, every creative endeavor contributes to my unleashed destiny. This newfound sense of purpose has transformed my life. I am a mentor/coach to others, sharing my story and encouraging others to find meaning in their own lives. My journey has taught me that life is not about grand, sweeping changes, but about the small, everyday actions that collectively define who we are and what we become. Just as epsilon in mathematics ensures precision and truth, the seemingly insignificant moments in life are essential in creating a meaningful and purposeful *Unleashed* **Destiny**.

Ex·hale

to emit breath or vapor; breathe out; to let or force out of the lungs...

Today, I decide to exhale and breathe out unwanted thoughts so that I can re-focus my attention on what's important right now.

Every breath I take is in gratitude for this very moment which allows me to breathe in wellness and wholeness so that I can exhale all that doesn't serve me.

Today, I decide to exhale doubt and inhale confidence. I will no longer hold my breath waiting for the day I can feel comfortable with loving "who I am, when I am, where I am."

Beloved it's time to exhale the past...Despite the peaceful life I was living with my husband and son, I always felt as though I was holding my breath, waiting for a moment that would allow me to exhale and truly walk in my *unleashed* **destiny**. There was a deep desire within my soul to make a difference in the world. As a passionate warrior teacher, a profession I absolutely love, I often felt that I needed to ascend towards excellence and be or do something that would leave a lasting impact on my students, coworkers and friends. However, "life be life-in" and my responsibilities of home, family, work, church, and my fear of stepping into the unknown kept me from pursuing my true calling.

There deep within me was turmoil- holding my breath, unable to fully embrace my **destiny**. "In mathematics, epsilon represents a very small, positive quantity. It is used to define limits and ensure precision.

Just like epsilon, small actions and decisions, though seemingly insignificant, play a crucial role in guiding us to our destiny. It's in these tiny, almost imperceptible moments that we find our true path."

When does **Destiny** Need An Intervention? The defining moment I was ready to exhale and step into my destiny, not overlooking the importance of the small, consistent steps I could take every day was when I decided to focus on my "epsilon moment." Hence, I answered the call to become a co-author of Amazon's best-selling anthology, "When **Destiny** Needs An Intervention."

I invested in *When Destiny Needs An Intervention, Volumes 1, 2, and 3* to write and share my signature stories of healing from the pain, shame and fear of being sexually molested at the age of 13 years old. I inhaled joy, peace and love and exhaled addiction, codependency and depression, through vulnerability, transparency and accountability. For three years, I put in the work of being comfortable with being uncomfortable as I began to heal from my trauma as a child. I realized my silence was not golden and I needed to reclaim my **destiny**. Each of my actions, though small, was intentional, and they brought me immense joy and a sense of purpose. As I continue to embrace these epsilon moments, there has been a shift within.

I no longer feel like I'm holding my breath, waiting for the right time to exhale. Instead, I choose breathing deeply and fully, with mindfulness practices, walking and knowing that each small step is guiding me closer to my *unleashed* **destiny.** My journey has had a ripple effect that positively impacts my personal health and well-being. My physical health started with me practicing and developing healthy habits and routines like prayer, devotion, walking, stretching, eating healthy foods, drinking water, and getting 8-10 hours of restful sleep. My mental health which was full of stress, anxiety, and depression now involves mindfulness, meditation, therapy and journaling which give me mental clarity and emotional stability. Because of my increased energy, my new healthy living now boosts my energy levels, making it easier for me to engage in these daily activities and pursue my personal wellness goals with greater enthusiasm.

My relationships, social connections, personal, professional, spiritual development and growth have led to me prioritizing and enhancing my life so that I can continue to contribute to having a broader- more positive impact in my community, society, and for my legacy and future generations. Just as the epsilon symbol ensures precision in mathematics, the moments I create will ensure that I am aligned with my true purpose.

Conclusion

By embracing and valuing each step, I find fulfillment and MY *unleashed* **destiny** of what I have been waiting for. This essence of waiting to exhale, symbolizes the anticipation of release and relief. I have had to hold my breath, while enduring the difficult moments and challenges of life. As I waited for the calm and prayed for God's peace, I can finally exhale and let go of all that weighs me down.

Ad·dic·tion

"I never knew the weight, until I felt the Freedom."
—Rochelle D. Jacobs (*When Destiny Needs An Intervention, Vol.2* **For the Love of Money**)

Addiction is a complex and chronic condition characterized by the compulsive use of a substance or engagement in a behavior despite harmful consequences. It involves a physical and psychological dependence on a substance or activity, leading to significant disruptions in various aspects of an individual's life, including health, relationships, and daily functioning.

How did I end up here at this end of the road? I was known by my infectious laughter and a spirit that seemed destined for greatness. I had quite the talent for doing all the things, saying YES to everyone and everything! However, behind the radiant smile, I carried a heavy burden. After being sexually molested at the age of 13- I soon turned to sugary sweets-honey buns, ice cream, cookies and brownies, oh my, to cope with the pressures of life. What began as an occasional escape gradually tightened its grip, becoming a daily necessity. My addiction, initially hidden, began to creep into every aspect of my life, dimming my destiny. The attempt to escape from my pain- only created more pain. The effects of my unresolved trauma were devastating! It affected my negative habits and obscured my outlook on life, all roads led to my sugar addiction and poor decision-making. It took a toll on my life and interpersonal relationships. It triggered real physical pain, symptoms, and disease especially when I found myself having Covid in 2021.

As the days and years passed, my dreams of becoming a motivational speaker, and to escape the sidelines of complacency seemed to slip further out of reach. My days were spent in a sugary haze and my nights in painful, regretful turmoil. The sugary delights that once promised relief now held me captive, their chains growing heavier with each passing day. My finances, relationships, personal and spiritual development once full of life and passion, grew darker, mirroring my internal struggle with a range of self-destructive behaviors.

I watched helplessly as my potential to live my extraordinary, best life was swallowed by my sugar ad-

-diction. I decided to seek help, support and encouragement, from a therapist because the grip of my demons was strong. After choosing the comfort of my sugar addiction, I found myself alone-stressed out binge eating a whole sheet cake instead of embracing the pain of facing my harsh reality- I was a sugar addict and for the first time, I began to confront the emptiness that had taken over my life. As I lay in bed with tears streaming down my face, I realized how far I'd strayed from my path towards destiny. This sugar addiction had not only stolen my future but also my present, leaving me with a profound sense of loss and regret.

I used to start my mornings with glazed donuts, honey buns or cinnamon rolls thinking I was treating myself. Little did I know, these indulgences were setting the stage for a series of health challenges such as weight gain, high blood pressure, inflammation and high cholesterol! At first, I didn't notice much. The rush of sugar gave me a quick burst of energy, but soon after, I'd crash, feeling sluggish and irritable. Over time, my weight began creeping up, and my energy levels became unpredictable. I didn't connect the dots until a routine check-up revealed high blood sugar levels. My doctor warned about the risks of developing insulin resistance and type 2 diabetes if I didn't change my habits.

It was a wake-up call, but breaking free from my sugar cravings was harder than I expected. I slowly began to reduce my sugar intake and started noticing small improvements. My energy stabilized, and I lost weight. However, the real challenge came when I realized how deeply sugar had influenced my eating habits. Snacks, desserts, even seemingly healthy foods were laden with hidden sugars.

"**Sugar because I'm tired**— because there's simply too much to do and no way to do it. **Sugar because it's fast**— and I need 30 more minutes of strength. **Sugar because I'm lonely**— because something sweet tastes like human touch feels. **Sugar because it's cheap**— one buck instead of five. **Sugar because I didn't plan**— didn't take time to prep to stand against the current. **Sugar because I'm sad**— about so many things, and for two seconds I can forget. **Sugar because I don't want to move**— and sugar sits here with me. **Sugar because I'm scared**— of what might pull me if I were fit. **Sugar because I'm so angry**— I don't care what happens. **Sugar because I'm ashamed**— of how far I've let it go already."

—Author Unknown

It took dedication and mindfulness to reshape my diet. I swapped sugary drinks for water and herbal teas and traded processed snacks for fruits and nuts. Gradually, my taste buds adjusted, and I began appreciating the natural sweetness of foods. Months later, I visited my doctor for a follow-up. My blood sugar levels had improved, and I was no longer at risk for diabetes. The journey wasn't easy, but reclaiming my health and vitality was worth every effort.

Looking back, I now understand how sugar had silently contributed to my health challenges. It taught me the importance of mindful eating and listening to my body's needs. Today, I'm grateful for the opportunity to enjoy a balanced diet that supports my well-being without compromising my health. In this moment of clarity, I decided to no longer let my sugar addiction define ME.

I asked for help by utilizing my health insurance and found a qualified emotional eating therapist with the EAP (employee assistance program). Oh, the journey was excruciating, marked by withdrawals, therapy sessions, and the constant temptation to return to my old ways of coping. My focus word became perseverance, driven by the flicker of hope that had sparked within.

During my recovery, I discovered a love for walking and journaling. This became my form of therapy, a way to express the pain and hope I was feeling. Slowly, but surely, taking small steps in my healing journey. Each investment in my own self care practices was a step closer to being set free from the chains of addiction.

With every doctor's visit and check-up, my face lights up with admiration and inspiration which fills me with a profound sense of accomplishment and peace. As I reflect and remember finding myself coming face to face with a neon light flashing "END OF THE ROAD!" and having to decide which direction to go, I am grateful that God gave me the strength and the will to fight my way out of the darkness of sugar addiction, so that I could reclaim my life and my **destiny**.

The journey wasn't easy, but my story is a testament to my strength and resilience. I pray as you read this book that you see it as a beacon of light, especially if you are struggling with an addiction- i.e. drugs, alcohol, or sugar. Because beloved, it's never too late to reclaim your life and *unleash* your true **destiny**. Addiction is a treatable condition, and recovery is possible with appropriate support, intervention, and a commitment to change. I have learned that the path to my dreams was not a straight line, but a winding road filled with challenges.

I was determined to overcome my challenges, so that I could walk in my *unleashed* **destiny** by confronting my deepest fears and embracing inner strength.

Key aspects of addiction I learned

1. Compulsion and Craving
- **Compulsion:** An overwhelming urge to use the substance or engage in the behavior.
- **Craving:** Intense desire or urge for the substance or activity, often triggered by cues or stress.

2. Loss of Control
- **Inability to Stop:** Difficulty in controlling the use of the substance or engagement in the behavior, even when attempting to cut back or quit.
- **Excessive Use:** Consuming larger amounts or engaging in the behavior for longer periods than intended.

3. Dependence
- **Physical Dependence:** The body's adaptation to the substance, leading to tolerance (needing more of the substance to achieve the same effect) and withdrawal symptoms when not using it.
- **Psychological Dependence:** Emotional and mental preoccupation with the substance or activity, often using it to cope with stress, anxiety,

- or other negative emotions.

4. **Negative Consequences**
   - **Health Problems:** Physical and mental health issues resulting from substance use or behavior.
   - **Social and Interpersonal Issues:** Strained relationships, isolation, and conflicts arising from addiction.
   - **Occupational and Financial Problems:** Impaired performance at work or school, financial difficulties due to spending on the substance or activity.

5. **Persistence Despite Harm**
   - **Continued Use:** Ongoing use of the substance or engagement in the behavior despite awareness of its harmful effects and adverse consequences. Types of Addiction
   - **Substance Addiction:** Includes addiction to alcohol, drugs (both legal and illegal), and nicotine.
   - **Behavioral Addiction:** Involves compulsive engagement in behaviors such as gambling, gaming, shopping, eating, and internet use.

Treatment and Recovery

- **Therapy and Counseling**: Cognitive-behavioral therapy (CBT), motivational interviewing, and other therapeutic approaches.
- **Medication:** For certain addictions, medications can help manage withdrawal symptoms and reduce cravings.
- **Support Groups:** Peer support groups like Alcoholics Anonymous (AA) and Narcotics Anonymous (NA).
- **Lifestyle Changes:** Developing healthier coping mechanisms, establishing a supportive environment, and engaging in meaningful activities.

10 Steps
to overcome sugar addiction

1. **Awareness and Education:** Understand the effects of sugar on the body and recognize signs of addiction, such as cravings, mood swings, and energy crashes.

2. **Gradual Reduction:** Start by gradually reducing sugar intake. Identify sources of added sugars in your diet, such as sugary drinks, sweets, and processed foods, and begin replacing them with healthier alternatives.

3. **Read Labels:** Pay attention to food labels and ingredient lists. Sugar can be disguised under various names like sucrose, high-fructose corn syrup, and dextrose. Choose foods with lower sugar content or no added sugars.

4. **Eat Whole Foods:** Focus on whole foods such as fruits, vegetables, lean proteins, and whole grains. These foods provide essential nutrients without the added sugars found in processed foods.

5. **Stay Hydrated:** Sometimes, dehydration can mimic feelings of hunger or cravings for sugary foods. Drink plenty of water throughout the day to stay hydrated and reduce cravings.

6. **Manage Stress:** Stress can trigger cravings for comfort foods, including sugary treats. Practice stress-reducing techniques such as deep breathing, meditation, yoga, or hobbies to manage stress levels effectively.

7. **Get Enough Sleep:** Lack of sleep can disrupt hunger hormones and increase cravings for sugary foods. Aim for 7-9 hours of quality sleep each night to support overall health and reduce cravings.

8. **Seek Support:** Consider joining a support group or working with a healthcare professional, such as a registered dietitian or therapist, who specializes in addiction and nutrition. They can provide guidance, encouragement, and personalized strategies to overcome sugar addiction.

9. **Practice Mindful Eating:** Pay attention to hunger and fullness cues, and eat meals and snacks mindfully. Choose foods that nourish your body and satisfy your cravings without relying on sugar.

10. **Celebrate Progress:** Recognize and celebrate small victories along the way. Overcoming sugar addiction is a journey that requires persistence and commitment, so be kind to yourself and celebrate each step toward a healthier lifestyle.

Conclusion

Sugar addiction can be challenging due to its pervasive presence in many foods and its addictive qualities. By implementing these steps and making gradual changes, you can reduce sugar cravings, improve your overall health, and break free from sugar addiction over time.

Strong·hold

"Your mind is a **"stronghold"**, and what you feed it determines what kind of stronghold it becomes. Feed it well."

—Michael Hyatt

In life, we all face strongholds that try to imprison us, robbing us of our peace, joy, and sense of safety. I've encountered two such moments that challenged my resilience and forced me to confront the depths of despair. These experiences, while incredibly painful, also became pivotal points in my journey toward reclaiming my **destiny.**

S - Shackles

Fear and overwhelming sadness became the "shackles" binding me after I was robbed of my cherished possessions. One ordinary morning, as I was walking to work, my sense of normalcy was shattered. A stranger, while riding his bike, forcefully snatched my gold chain from around my neck. The empty space on my neck mirrored the emptiness that settled in my heart.

The experience left me feeling vulnerable and stripped of security.

T - Thorns

However, this wasn't the only instance where I felt robbed. A much deeper wound was inflicted on my soul when I was sexually molested at the age of thirteen. This act of betrayal and violation was more than just a physical intrusion; it pierced my heart with "thorns" of mistrust, shattered and innocence stolen. What should have been a safe space, surrounded by friends and loved ones, turned into a labyrinth of fear and confusion.

R - Robbed

In both instances, I was "robbed"-Robbed of my sense of security, my peace, and my trust. These moments became dark shadows, trying to envelop my spirit. It's easy to feel hopeless when what you cherish is snatched away. The weight of carrying these experiences was heavy, often leaving me questioning my worth and my future. These offenses of robbery and assault charges kept me from my destiny because they created significant barriers that limited my potential and hindered my growth. I developed a fixed mindset and resisted change and growth- afraid to take risks and embrace new challenges that were crucial for my personal development. Holding onto grudges and unresolved conflicts robbed and consumed my emotional energy, leaving me empty-having a less than capacity for pursuing positive goals and relationships. My feelings of depression and hopelessness made it difficult for me to envision and work toward my unleashed destiny. Habitual procrastination prevented me from taking timely action on important tasks and goals, resulting in missed opportunities and stagnation. The idea of being robbed left me P.O.O.R (passing over opportunities repeatedly) by self-sabotaging and engaging in behaviors that only undermined my destiny of success, trying to be perfect, over-committing, and avoiding responsibilities, which only derailed my progress and prevented me from achieving my goals.

O - Obstacles

Yet, these strongholds became my greatest teachers. They were the "**obstacles**" I needed to overcome to find my strength. Each tear shed and every moment of grief was a step toward building resilience. *"Acknowledge the pain but refuse to let it define you."* This became my mantra as I climbed the mountain of recovery, determined to reclaim what was robbed from me—not the jewelry, but my spirit and my sense of self-worth.

N - Nets

My journey wasn't solitary. I found support in unexpected places—friends, therapy, and my own writing. The words, my thoughts and feelings written in my journals became my "**nets**", catching the fragments of my broken self and weaving them into a tapestry of healing and empowerment.

G - Gratification

The "**gratification**" of navigating through these dark periods was profound. Confronting and understanding the shadows of my past, and realizing they no longer had power over me, brought a deep sense of satisfaction. The journey of healing allowed me to reclaim my power and find joy again.

H - Hurdles

Gradually, what seemed like insurmountable "**hurdles**" became milestones of progress. Every small victory, be it a day without flashbacks or a moment of laughter, was a testament to my strength and resilience.

O - Overcomer

Overcoming these strongholds requires self-awareness, support, and a commitment to personal development and positive change. I had to Own It! I had to own my overwhelming fear and anxiety that was paralyzing my decision-making and lead to my avoidance behaviors. My fear robbed me of stepping out of my comfort zone.

L - Labor Pains

Navigating through these "labor pains" of healing, I found clarity. Every twist and turn taught me more about myself, granting me the power to reshape my future. The journey is ongoing, and every new path is a kaizen step toward wholeness.

D - Destiny

Robbed but not defeated, my "destiny" awaited. By confronting these strongholds and robbers of my peace, I found the strength to reclaim my life. I turned pain into purpose, fear into fuel, and brokenness into beauty. My journey is a testament that you-Beloved, can rise- from the ashes, stronger and more determined than ever.

S - Self and Soul Care

Sugar was my stronghold and I found myself in a sticky situation of having powerful and persistent cravings- and a co-dependence on sugary foods and beverages. Oh the overwhelming control that sugar cravings had on my eating habits and overall health. I developed intense cravings and frequent desires to consume sugary foods, which often lead to overconsumption. My dependency on sugar-those strong feeling of needing that "fix" or sugar high to feel satisfied or to cope with my emotional states of stress, anxiety, or sadness was overwhelming. I began taking intentional steps to break free from its grip, so that I could improve my health, well-being, and quality of life.

Guided by *"self and soul care"*, I continue to move forward. Taking care of myself holistically—mentally, emotionally, and spiritually—has become an anchor in my life. Practicing self-care and nurturing my soul has provided the foundation for lasting healing and growth. My story is not one of defeat but of triumph, a journey through darkness to find the enduring light. I share these experiences not to dwell on the pain but to illuminate the path for others who may find themselves in similar struggles.

Stronghold Characteristics of Old Ways and Behaviors

1. **Resistance to Change:** A reluctance or refusal to adapt to new ideas, methods, or situations.
2. **Comfort Zone Dependence:** Preferring familiar routines and environments over exploring new possibilities.
3. **Negative Patterns:** Persisting in habits and behaviors that are counterproductive or harmful.
4. **Fixed Mindset:** Believing that abilities and intelligence are static and cannot be developed, leading to avoidance of challenges.
5. **Fear of the Unknown:** Anxiety or fear about the uncertainty and risks associated with change.

Impact on Personal *Destiny*

1. **Stagnation:** Remaining in old habits and behaviors prevents growth, learning, and progress, leading to a stagnant life.
2. **Missed Opportunities:** Resistance to change can cause individuals to miss out on new opportunities for personal, professional, and social development.
3. **Unfulfilled Potential:** Adhering to outdated behaviors and mindsets can prevent individuals from realizing their full potential.
4. **Relationship Strain:** Inflexibility and resistance to change can create tension and conflict in relationships, as others may grow and evolve.
5. **Mental Health Issues:** Chronic resistance to change can lead to feelings of frustration, anxiety, and depression.

The stronghold of old ways and behaviors can significantly impede personal growth and the fulfillment of one's destiny. Overcoming this stronghold requires self-awareness, a growth mindset, setting clear goals, incremental change, learning and adaptation, seeking support, reflecting on progress, and challenging negative thoughts. By actively working to replace outdated behaviors and thought patterns with new, positive ones, individuals can unlock their full potential and pursue their true destiny with confidence and determination.

Strongholds in life often refer to deeply ingrained patterns or obstacles that can significantly impact one's well-being and growth. Some common examples include:

1. **Fear:** Persistent anxiety or phobias that hinder progress and personal development.
2. **Shame:** Deep-seated feelings of unworthiness or guilt that affect self-esteem and relationships.
3. **Addiction:** Dependency on substances or behaviors that disrupt daily life and health.
4. **Negative Thought Patterns:** Chronic negative thinking that affects one's outlook and decision-making.
5. **Unforgiveness:** Holding onto grudges or resentments that can poison relationships and personal peace.
6. **Pride:** An inflated sense of self that can lead to isolation and hinder personal growth.
7. **Trauma:** Unresolved past experiences that continues to affect current emotions and behaviors.
8. **Doubt:** Lack of confidence in oneself or one's abilities, preventing the pursuit of goals.

9. **Depression:** Persistent sadness or lack of motivation that impacts daily functioning.
10. **Anger:** Uncontrolled anger that can damage relationships and cause personal turmoil.

Conclusion

Addressing these strongholds often involves self-awareness, seeking support, and developing strategies to overcome them. "Oh, but the struggle is real"- sometimes we won't change until the pain of where we are exceeds the pain of change. Feeling stuck in certain patterns of harmful behavior keeps us from moving forward. Stop applying an old formula to a new level. Today, you get to decide to change the formula you apply to your life if you want to get a different result.

Heal·ing

"Healing is a journey, not a destination. Every step forward counts, no matter how small."

—Author Unknown

It was the start of a warm, radiant summer that I was filled with joy, eagerly anticipating a long, extended visit to a friend's house. I wanted desperately to escape the uncertainty at my own home to seek solace, a place of laughter, and friendships. Never would I imagine a storm would come in the form of being sexually molested by someone I once trusted. The lightning strike was the manifestation of betrayal and abuse that left me with a deep fear and lingering shame. As the years went by, the wounds healed on the surface, but deep inside, I carried an ember of pain, hidden beneath layers of resilience. This internal scar mirrored the lasting impact of being deceived by a loved one, similar to the betrayal felt when lied to by my spouse years later. The lie was overshadowed by wild thorns and tangled vines. These thorns symbolized the emotional wounds, while the tangled vines represented...

the web of deceit and broken promises- and was determined to reclaim my sanctuary of healing. My first step was to clear the overgrowth. This echoed the process of confronting and acknowledging my past traumas, akin to revisiting those painful summer memories in therapy. Each thorn removed was a memory revisited and understood as a step toward healing from the molestation. It wasn't easy; the pain was raw and visceral. But through the process, I learned to acknowledge the betrayal without letting it define my spirit. I came to understand that the shadows from my ugly past were not my fault and that true strength came from facing the pain and shame head-on. I now know that silence is not golden when it hides pain. I had to speak out about my sexual molestation so that I could begin healing and reclaiming my voice. I pray beloved that by acknowledging and sharing my story that it will empower you, to process your own trauma and begin to heal.

"I could not meet God in my revival until I met him in my Brokenness."
*—Rochelle D. Jacobs (**When Destiny Needs An Intervention, Vol.3** For the Love of Brokenness)*

As the years continued to go by I encountered a massive, deeply rooted thorn—the thorn of unforgiveness. This thorn in my side represented the deep-seated hurt and betrayal caused by the husband's lies. Having this thorn removed was no small feat, just as finding the strength to forgive seemed insurmountable. With patience and perseverance, the soul began to seek the root cause of my pain and suffering, during my therapeutic sessions—moments of understanding, compassion, and eventually, the decision to let go and forgive myself and my spouse-slowly but surely, the thorn was removed, and in its place, celebration of forgiveness became my spiritual weapon. I forgave with mercy and not malice- this symbolized the beginning of having a fresh perspective—a deliberate choice to let go of resentment and to heal-nurturing my new way of thinking involved daily acts of self-care, moments of reflection, and exercises in gratitude. I was committed to building positive habits and focusing on its future.

As time passed, my soul thrived, having turned a landscape of pain into a haven of healing and purpose. It stood as a testament to the power of forgiveness, the resilience of the human spirit, and the incredible beauty that emerges when one dares to heal and embrace their true **destiny**.

Conclusion

During my work in therapy, I gathered the courage to release my anger and resentment by journaling- realizing these were chains that bound my soul. The scars of my past were still there, but they were now symbols of my incredible journey through transformation. I learned to forgive my husband, who had wronged me- it was not for his peace but for my own.

A happy heart is good medicine and a joyful mind causes healing...

—Proverbs 17:22

Ex·traor·di·nar·y

My "extraordinary" journey post-Covid is not just of survival, but of transformation in mind, body, and spirit. From a young age, I had always dreamed of soaring high above the clouds, exploring the vast world beyond the sky's horizons. This dream was, however, shrouded by trials and tribulations that demanded every bit of my resilience and courage. I'm reminded in the book of Isaiah 40:31 "But those who wait for the Lord [who expect, look for, and hope in Him]

Will gain new strength and renew their power; They will lift up their wings [and rise up close to God] like eagles [rising toward the sun]; They will run and not become weary, They will walk and not grow tired." The woman you see now, Rochelle D. Jacobs, started her journey as an inquisitive hatchling. In my early years, I overcame the dark shadows cast by past traumas, slowly nursing broken wings. As time passed, the flickering flames of my spirit grew stronger, marking the beginning of my "*Unleashed* **Destiny**."

Transformation of the Mind

The first steps in my transformation journey began in 1992 at Texas Southern University in Houston, Texas- Go Tigers! This journey took me 29 years, as I worked several jobs, taking night classes and then eventually dropping out in 2005. In 2006-2008, I attended ITT Technical Institute graduating with a 4.0 as valedictorian with an Associate's degree in Computer Network Systems.

Life continued to greet me with various hardships and obstacles, which led to me finally being sick and tired of living paycheck to paycheck, so I re-enrolled at TSU in the fall of 2017. The classes were all online which enabled me to continue to work as an hourly PE Teacher at Everest Academy. I am so proud of the work I accomplished in the next 4 years. I graduated Cum Laude, with as BS in Health Studies. Post-Covid, I have been honing my craft and passion for writing, pouring my thoughts and experiences into the written word. I am a 4x Amazon best-selling author. I pray that my story resonates with many of my readers and inspire others to embark on their own journeys of self-discovery.

Transformation of the Body

Wellness is a lifestyle, not an event- is a mantra I live by. It started with a "reset" challenge that concluded with me successfully releasing 20 lbs of unwanted weight. Eating clean and staying hydrated was my "fountain of youth" as I embraced my "50th" birthday. I am dedicated to becoming wholly well physically, mentally, and spiritually by shedding the weight of my past as I continue to ascend towards excellence. "Every day and every way I'm soaring higher, and higher, and higher and you better believe it!"

Transformation of the Spirit

My spiritual transformation is perhaps the most profound. I embarked on a radical journey with the ME 2.0 program-"12 Dimensions of Wellness", an investment that broadened my horizons and deepened my understanding of self. Each dimension offered a piece of wisdom that nourished my soul, rekindling the inner flame with renewed vigor. Amidst this spiritual journey, I have discovered that "Self-Care Is The New Sexy" through the joy of travel to the beautiful island of St. Marten. The international flight across the world had my spirit soaring with the beauty of God's deep, inner peace that cemented my spiritual transformation.

An **"extraordinary"** life is uniquely defined by individual passions, dreams, and circumstances, creating a tapestry of profound fulfillment, purpose, and joy.

10 Key Elements
of an Extraordinary Life

1. Passion and Purpose
Description: Living with a sense of direction and meaning. An extraordinary life often involves pursuing what you love and what gives you a profound sense of purpose. Examples: Following a career you're passionate about, engaging in activities that align with your values, and contributing to causes that matter to you.

2. Continuous Growth
Description: Committing to personal and professional development. An extraordinary life involves a dedication to lifelong learning and self-improvement. Examples: Reading, taking courses, attending workshops, seeking mentorship, and pushing personal boundaries.

3. Positive Relationships
Description: Fostering deep, meaningful connections with friends, family, and loved ones. An extraordinary life is enriched by a network of supportive and loving relationships. Examples: Spending quality time with loved ones, building strong friendships, and being part of a community.

4. Health and Wellness
Description: Prioritizing physical, mental, and emotional well-being. An extraordinary life often includes maintaining a balanced lifestyle to support overall health. Examples: Regular exercise, healthy eating, mental health practices like meditation, and seeking joy and laughter.

5. Financial Freedom
Description: Achieving financial stability and independence. An extraordinary life often features effective financial management that allows freedom and choice. Examples: Saving, investing wisely, living within means, and feeling secure about the future.

6. Adventure and Exploration

Description: Embracing new experiences, cultures, and pursuits. An extraordinary life includes a spirit of curiosity and adventure.

Examples: Traveling, trying new hobbies, learning new skills, and seeking out new challenges.

7. Giving Back

Description: Contributing to others and making a positive impact. An extraordinary life is often marked by generosity and a commitment to helping others.

Examples: Volunteering, mentoring, philanthropy, and community service.

8. Living Authentically

Description: Being true to oneself and living in alignment with personal values and beliefs. An extraordinary life involves embracing your true identity.

Examples: Expressing yourself freely, making choices based on personal convictions, and trusting your intuition.

9. Joy and Gratitude

Description: Finding joy in everyday moments and practicing gratitude. An extraordinary life celebrates the small, beautiful moments and acknowledges the positive.

Examples: Keeping a gratitude journal, relishing simple pleasures, and celebrating successes, big and small.

10. Peace and Balance

Description: Striving for balance and inner peace. An extraordinary life involves managing stress, maintaining harmony in various life aspects, and seeking tranquility.

Examples: Setting boundaries, prioritizing self-care, practicing mindfulness, and finding time to relax and rejuvenate.

If you would indulge me let me paint a picture of what an extraordinary life looks like:

Imagine waking up each day with excitement and purpose, eagerly anticipating the day's activities. You have built a career around your passion, and it enables you to make a meaningful impact in the world.

You dedicate time to grow and learn, attending master classes and exploring new fields of interest. Your health is vibrant because you prioritize physical activity, nutritious food, and mental wellness practices.

Your life is filled with deep and loving relationships, where support and joy abound. You enjoy financial freedom, which allows you to pursue your hobbies and passions without stress.

You seek out adventure, traveling to new places and embracing diverse cultures. Your compassionate heart leads you to give back to your community, making a tangible difference in the lives of others.

Most importantly, you live authentically and in harmony with your values, finding joy in every moment and maintaining a balance that brings inner peace. Your life is a testament to the extraordinary, filled with passion, growth, love, health, adventure, generosity, authenticity, gratitude, and peace.

Conclusion

Beloved, by embracing these elements, your journey through "*Unleashed* **Destiny**" can become the tapestry of an extraordinary life, uniquely tailored to your experiences, dreams, and passions.

Des·tin·y

Destiny is defined as a concept that refers to the idea that our lives are predetermined by some higher force or fate. While some people believe in destiny, others believe that we have the power to shape our own lives through our choices and actions. Regardless of your beliefs, there may be times when you feel like your life is out of control, or that you are not living up to your potential. This can be a sign that an intervention is needed to help you find your power, purpose, and prosperity. *When does **Destiny** need an Intervention? Right Now!*

Here are some signs that your Destiny needs an Intervention:

1. **You feel stuck or stagnant in your life:** If you feel like you're not making progress towards your goals, or that you're not growing as a person, it may be time for an intervention.

2. **You're experiencing a lot of negativity:** If you're feeling depressed, anxious, or overwhelmed by negative

thoughts and emotions, an intervention may be necessary to help you overcome these challenges.

3. You're facing significant life changes: If you're going through a divorce, a job loss, or another major life change, an intervention can help you navigate these challenges and find a new path forward.

4. You're struggling with addiction or other destructive behaviors: If you're engaging in behaviors that are harming yourself or others, an intervention can be a powerful tool to help you overcome these challenges and find a healthier way of living.

If any of these signs resonate with you, it may be time to seek out an intervention. This could involve working with a therapist, coach, or other professional to help you identify your goals, develop a plan of action, and stay accountable to your progress.

Remember, you have the power to shape your own **destiny**. By taking control of your life and seeking out the help you need, you can find your power, purpose, and prosperity.

The moment my **Destiny** was *unleashed* I was filled with the power to reclaim my voice, walk on purpose and lead with passion to live in abundant prosperity and peace. The chains of doubt and conformity kept me fr-

-om embracing my own **destiny**. I realized with clarity that my path was not predetermined but a blank canvas awaiting bold and powerful strokes of my creation. I needed to unleash my inner power and let my aspirations soar beyond all limitations. Beloved, I encourage you to embrace the uniqueness that defines you; by embracing your distinct destiny, you unlock the extraordinary journey that awaits you. Become the architect of your fate, for within you is the potential to unleash a destiny uniquely yours. Your destiny awaits your courage, your passion, and your unwavering commitment to write a narrative that resonates with your true essence.

DESTINY

D – Decide
- Deciding to take control of your life and make purposeful choices.
- Pursuing your dreams and having a clear sense of direction in life.
- Discovering your passions, strengths, and true purpose.

E – Empowerment
- Feeling empowered to make decisions and take control of your life.
- Empowering yourself through knowledge, resilience, and self-belief.
- Executing your plans with determination and action to achieve your goals.

S – Self-Care
- Prioritizing self-care to maintain your physical, mental and emotional well-being.
- Commitment to ongoing personal and professional and spiritual growth.

T – Transformation
- Transforming challenges into opportunities and evolving continuously
- Transcend limitations and achieve greatest potential.

I – Inspiration
- Inspiring others with your journey and experiences.
- Living intentionally and aligning your actions with your core values and goals.

N – Nurturing Relationships
- Nurturing your mind, body, and spirit through self-care and wellness practices.
- Having the strength to say 'no' to distractions and commitments that don't serve your purpose.

Y – Yes
- Seeking new experiences and exploring the unknown with curiosity and enthusiasm.
- Being open to saying 'yes' to opportunities and experiences that align with your destiny.

Destiny Affirmations

Destiny affirmations are statements designed to affirm and align your life with a positive, purposeful destiny. I pray that these affirmations are meant to empower your positive mindset, encourage your personal growth, and support your belief that your Unleashed Destiny is shaped by your intention and action.

"I attract opportunities that align perfectly with my destiny."

"Every challenge I face is a steppingstone toward greatness."

"I am worthy of living a life of purpose, joy, and fulfillment."

"I am breaking free from fear and embracing the power within."

"My destiny unfolds with every courageous step I take."

"I release old limitations and welcome new opportunities."

"Each day, I align my actions with my true purpose and passion."

"I am empowered to create the life I envision with confidence."

"I radiate positivity and attract positivity into my life."

"I am the architect of my destiny, and I choose greatness."

Citations & References

Aghedo, Karla J: H3W (Houston Wellness Workshops for Women) https://karlajaghedo.com/Executive Wellness Mindset Coach/Investment Club/SisStore Joy Christian Book Store/ https://sisstorejoy.com/home

Bible gateway. Amplified Version / King James Version. All scripture references are Retrieved from https://www.biblegateway.com/Amplified-Version-King James-Version-Bible/

Blume, Judy. (2001). Are you there God? It's me, Margaret. New York: Atheneum Books for Young Readers

Good Reads Quotes: All quotes are retrieved from https://www.goodreads.com/quotes

Lewis, S. D. (2018). Get your life: A 90 day journal. Create Space Independent Publishing Platform.

Lewis, S. (2020). Get your life: The blueprint. Shana D. Lewis LLC.

Lewis, Shana Denise: Get Your Life: The 90 Day Journal; Get Your Life: The Blueprint YXL (Your Extraordinary Life) Academy https://www.facebook.com/groups/yxlacademy/ ME2.0 (12 Dimensions of Wellness) Executive Wellness Coach https://www.shanadlewis.com/

Lewis, Shana D. (Visionary.) (2021-2023). Anthology: When destiny Needs An Intervention. Vol. 1, 2, 3: SDL Enterprises, LLC

Merriam-Webster's online dictionary (11th ed.) All definitions used in this book are retrieved from https://www.merriam-webster.com/dictionary

Moore, Beth. (2007). A woman's heart: God's dwelling place. Life Way Press.

Psychology Today. All Strategies, Techniques and Resources are retrieved from https://www.psychologytoday.com/us/basics/health

Speake, Wendy. (2019). Sugar Poem: The 40 day sugar fast. Baker Books. https://wendyspeake.com/40-day-feast/

Important Help lines and Websites

Mental Health Support
Texas:
Texas Health and Human Services
Phone: 1-888-963-7111
Website: hhs.texas.gov | https://www.hhs.texas.gov/

Rape Trauma Support
Texas:
Texas Association against Sexual Assault (TAASA):
Phone: 1-512-474-7190
Website: taasa.org | https://taasa.org/

Global:
RAINN (Rape, Abuse & Incest National Network):
Phone: 1-800-656-HOPE (4673)
Website: rainn.org | https://www.rainn.org/

Suicide Prevention
Texas:
Texas Suicide Prevention Council:
 Phone: 1-800-273-8255 (National Suicide Prevention Lifeline)
Website:texassuicideprevention.org|
https://texassuicideprevention.org

Domestic Abuse Support
Texas:
Texas Council on Family Violence:
Phone: 1-800-799-7233 (National Domestic Violence Hotline)
Website: tcfv.org | https://tcfv.org/

Violence Prevention
Texas:
Texas Department of Family and Protective Services:
Phone: 1-800-252-5400
Website: dfps.state.tx.us | https://www.dfps.state.tx.us/

Online/Web-Based
1. Better Help
Services: Accessible online therapy, including specializations in trauma
Website: betterhelp.com | https://www.betterhelp.com/

2. Talk space
Services: Online therapy sessions with licensed therapists experienced in trauma
Website: talkspace.com | https://www.talkspace.com/

About the Author

Rochelle D. Jacobs is an Amazon Best Selling author, empowerment coach, professional development facilitator, educator, motivational speaker, and podcast host. Rochelle has captivated audiences at the Refocus and Renew Houston Virtual Retreat hosted by Houston Wellness Workshops for Women, Creative Connections Conference, and the Comeback Champion Conference. She has been a guest on several podcasts such as: Book Talks with Sandy Sanders, Life Her Podcast, Coffee Conversations with Sandy & Friends and Wellness by Gretchen Podcast. Rochelle graduated cum laude from Texas Southern University with a Bachelor of Science in Health Studies, and class Valedictorian with an Associate's degree in Computer Network Systems at ITT Technical Institute in Houston, TX.

Rochelle has many roles: a Christian, wife, mother, sister, friend, servant, and physical education and health teacher. As a Destiny Interventionist Coach, Rochelle is passionate about teaching married women of faith, who are seeking inspiration, motivation and liberation from pain, fear, and shame of childhood sexual molestation, choose healing that will renew their joy, rebuild confidence and reclaim their voice. Her mission is to educate, equip, and empower women about the importance of investing in self and soul care through her podcast; **"Free Yourself Friyah"**; and online courses and master classes.

Rochelle is a life-long learner dedicated to achieving her full potential, advocating for inclusion, and remaining positive through even the most challenging trials. She uses her impressive skill set and her super power of Perseverance to increase her wellness knowledge and is always ascending towards excellence in mind, body, and spirit. She actively serves as the Communication Liaison for the Media Ministry Team, and is a Ladies Bible Class Teacher at her congregation, South Union Church of Christ. Rochelle lives in Houston, Texas and is married to John Jacobs with one son Marquise and a daughter Crystal Ekpin.

Ready to *unleash* your ***Destiny***?
Reach out to Rochelle using the QR code.

Made in the USA
Columbia, SC
19 November 2024